Especially for

_____

From

_____

Date

_____

© 2011 by Barbour Publishing, Inc.

ISBN 978-1-61626-160-3

Compiled by Snapdragon Editorial Group℠, Tulsa, OK.

Some selections are taken from *Girlfriend Connections: Moments of Laughter* by Bonnie Jensen, published by Barbour Publishing, Inc.

Scripture quotations marked KJV are taken from the King James Version of the Bible.

Scripture quotations marked NIV are taken from the HOLY BIBLE, NEW INTERNATIONAL VERSION®. NIV®. Copyright © 1973, 1978, 1984 by International Bible Society. Used by permission of Zondervan. All rights reserved.

Scripture quotations marked MSG are taken from *THE MESSAGE*. Copyright © by Eugene H. Peterson 1993, 1994, 1995, 1996, 2000, 2001, 2002. Used by permission of NavPress Publishing Group.

Scripture quotations marked CEV are from the Contemporary English Version, Copyright © 1991, 1992, 1995 by American Bible Society. Used by permission.

Scripture quotations marked NLT are taken from the *Holy Bible,* New Living Translation, copyright © 1996, 2004. Used by permission of Tyndale House Publishers, Inc. Wheaton, Illinois 60189, U.S.A. All rights reserved.

Published by Barbour Publishing, Inc., P.O. Box 719, Uhrichsville, Ohio 44683, www.barbourbooks.com

Our mission is to publish and distribute inspirational products offering exceptional value and biblical encouragement to the masses.

Member of the
Evangelical Christian
Publishers Association

Printed in China.

Moments of Laughter *for*
Girlfriends

*inspiration for
every day!*

BARBOUR
PUBLISHING

MAKE TIME FOR LAUGHTER

Make time for laughter with
your girlfriends every day.
Squeeze the joy out of every moment!

Day 2

MOUNTAINTOPS AND VALLEYS

A friend will joyfully sing with you when
you are on the mountaintop and silently
walk beside you through the valley.

UNKNOWN

Friendship Cements
the World

Friendship is the only cement that
will ever hold the world together.

WOODROW WILSON

THREE THINGS
TO DO DAILY

There are at least three things you
should do with your girlfriends daily:
Number one is laugh.
Number two is laugh.
And number three—that's right—laugh!

Love and Laughter

We cannot really love anybody with
whom we never laugh.

AGNES REPPLIER

Never Stop Laughing

We don't stop laughing because
we grow old; we grow old
because we stop laughing.

Michael Pritchard

LAUGHTER IMPROVES EVERYTHING

Laughter need not be cut out of anything,
since it improves everything.

BLESSED INFLUENCE

Blessed is the influence of one true,
loving human soul on another.

GEORGE ELIOT

Day
9

True Friendship

To like and dislike the same things,
that is indeed true friendship.

SALLUST

Day
10

SMILE!

A happy heart makes the face cheerful.

PROVERBS 15:13 NIV

The Cure-All

Girlfriends just know—the
combination of shopping, chocolate,
and lots of laughter is a guaranteed
cure for almost anything!

Nature's Masterpiece

A friend may well be reckoned the
masterpiece of Nature.

Ralph Waldo Emerson

TRUE HAPPINESS

True happiness consists not in
the multitude of friends,
but in their worth and choice.

SAMUEL JOHNSON

Day
14

LOVE REALIZED

It is a curious thought, but it is only when
you see people looking ridiculous that you
realize just how much you love them.

AGATHA CHRISTIE

Day
15

Happy Old Age

When grace is joined with
wrinkles, it is adorable.
There is an unspeakable dawn
in happy old age.

VICTOR HUGO

THE PRIZE

Girlfriends are the prize in
the cereal box of life.

Be Yourself

A real friend is not so much
someone you feel free to be
serious with as someone you
feel free to be silly with.

SYDNEY J. HARRIS

GIRLFRIEND MOTTO:

If every word I said could make
you laugh, I would talk forever.

A Day without Laughter

That day is lost on which
one has not laughed.

French Proverb

Day
20

LAUGHTER IS THE SPARK

Laughter is the spark of the soul.

UNKNOWN

Glory Begins
and Ends...

Think where man's glory
most begins and ends,
And say my glory was
I had such friends.

WILLIAM YEATS

SWEET SUPPORT

Thus nature has no love for solitude, and
always leans, as it were, on some support;
and the sweetest support is found in the
most intimate friendship.

MARCUS TULLIUS CICERO

Day
23

A True Friend

A true girlfriend laughs at
your stories even when
they're not funny.

FOREVER FRIENDS

With every friend I love who has been
taken into the brown bosom of the earth,
a part of me has been buried there;
but their contribution to my being of
happiness, strength, and understanding
remains to sustain me in an altered world.

HELEN KELLER

SIMPLE JOYS

The happiest days are spent appreciating
the simplest joys with your girlfriends.

LOVE YOURSELF

Friendship with oneself is all-important
because without it one cannot be friends
with anyone else in the world.

ELEANOR ROOSEVELT

Love through Friends

God supplies much of His love
through dearest friends.

Day
28

CHASE AWAY THE BLUES

Girlfriends have a way of bringing a smile
to our face on the bluest of days.

K. WILLIAMS

Day
29

Gentle Hugs

A smile gently hugs the heart
of the one who receives it.

UNKNOWN

BE THE SPARK!

Be the spark that ignites
your friends' laughter.

THANK YOU, LORD

Thank You, Lord, for the grace of
Your love, for the grace of friendship,
and for the grace of beauty.

HENRI J. M. NOUWEN

SPREAD HAPPINESS

Happiness is like jam.
You can't spread even a little without
getting some on yourself.

UNKNOWN

A Sweet Thing

It is a sweet thing,
friendship, a dear balm,
A happy and auspicious
bird of calm. . . .

PERCY BYSSHE SHELLEY

HAPPIEST MOMENTS

The happiest moments my heart knows
are those in which it is pouring forth its
affections to a few esteemed characters.

THOMAS JEFFERSON

Brighten a Day

Any day is sunny that is
brightened by a smile.

UNKNOWN

ALL THINGS FUN

Girlfriends always know how to
make the most dull outings fun.

COMMONALITIES

Friends have all things in common.

PLATO

Day
38

GOD IS GOOD

God is good all the time—and much of
the time His goodness is poured out into
our lives through the love, acceptance,
and laughter of friends.

The Reward of Friendship

The most I can do for my friend
is simply to be his friend.
I have no wealth to bestow on him.
If he knows that I am happy in loving
him, he will want no other reward.

HENRY DAVID THOREAU

SOLID

I do not wish to treat friendships daintily,
but with the roughest courage. When they
are real, they are not glass threads or
frost-work, but the solidest thing we know.

RALPH WALDO EMERSON

Joy and Laughter

*Our mouths were filled
with laughter, our tongues
with songs of joy.*

Psalm 126:2 NIV

FRIENDS CAN LAUGH
ABOUT ANYTHING

Girlfriends just know—the only
thing that outlasts a bad haircut
is the ability to laugh about it.

Shared Happiness

All who joy would win must share it.
Happiness was born a twin.

Lord Byron

LIKE DIAMONDS

Best friends are like diamonds,
precious but rare.

UNKNOWN

Like Sound Health

True friendship is like sound health;
the value of it is seldom known
until it be lost.

CHARLES CALEB COLTON

LAUGHTER IS A GIFT

Laughter is the gift of love,
the music of the soul.

Friends Make Life Worth Living

Each friend represents a world in us, a world possibly not born until they arrive, and it is only by this meeting that a new world is born.

ANAIS NIN

THE SWEETEST JOY

Friendship is one of the
sweetest joys of life.

CHARLES HADDON SPURGEON

ALWAYS THERE

A friend is one who walks
in when others walk out.

WALTER WINCHELL

THERE FOR YOU

A friend is someone who is there for you
when he'd rather be anywhere else.

LEN WEIN

God's Medicine

Mirth is God's medicine.
Everybody ought to bathe in it.

HENRY WARD BEECHER

Day
52

PERFECT JOY

Of no worldly good can the joy be perfect,
unless it is shared by a friend.

LATIN PROVERB

Walk Beside Me

Don't walk in front of me,
I may not follow.
Don't walk behind me, I may not lead.
Walk beside me and be my friend.

ALBERT CAMUS

ALWAYS TOGETHER

I don't remember how we
happened to meet each other.
I don't remember who got
along with whom first.
All I can remember is all
of us together—always.

UNKNOWN

A BEST FRIEND

A best friend is a sister that
destiny forgot to give you.

UNKNOWN

UNCONTROLLABLE LAUGHTER

Every now and then, it's delightful to
have the kind of laugh that makes your
stomach jiggle, that sends tears down
your face, and causes your eyes to
squint so it's impossible to see!

Like Rainbows

Girlfriends are like rainbows.
They brighten your life when
you've been through a storm.

EVERYONE IS BEAUTIFUL

Everyone is beautiful
when sharing laughter.

UNKNOWN

Friends Are Better than Fortunes

Good nature begets smiles,
smiles beget friends, and friends
are better than a fortune.

DAVID DUNN

THE ART OF HAPPINESS

The art of being happy lies
in the power of extracting
happiness from common things.

HENRY WARD BEECHER

THE SUNSHINE OF LIFE

Friends are the sunshine of life.

JOHN HAY

A Little Sunshine

Those who bring sunshine to the lives of
others cannot keep it from themselves.

SIR JAMES M. BARRIE

Joy in the Heart

Girlfriends put the fun
in together, the sad in apart,
and the joy in a heart.

Laughter Is Sunshine

Laughter is the sun that drives
winter from the face.

Victor Hugo

What the Heart Needs

A friend is what the heart
needs all the time.

HENRY VAN DYKE

BY-PRODUCT

Girlfriends create laughter—
it's a by-product of hearts that
are deeply connected and joined
together by a gracious God.

IN A MOMENT

Friendship is born at that moment when
one person says to another, "What!
You too? I thought I was the only one."

C. S. LEWIS

BE A FRIEND

Be a friend;
the rest will follow.

EMILY DICKINSON

share

*Laugh with your happy
friends when they're happy;
share tears when they're down.*

Romans 12:15 msg

NOW AND LATER

Girlfriends just know—
laugh now; laugh later.

Make Your Mark

If the essence of my being has caused a smile to have appeared upon your face or a touch of joy within your heart—then in living—I have made my mark.

THOMAS L. ODEM JR.

A GREAT LIFE

My father always used to say that when
you die, if you've got five real friends,
you've had a great life.

LEE IACOCCA

FRIENDSHIP BLOSSOMS

Friendship is not diminished by distance
or time, by imprisonment or war,
by suffering or silence. It is in these
things that it roots most deeply.
It is from these things that it flowers.

PAM BROWN

IMMEASURABLE VALUE

As we grow, the time between good bouts
of fun and laughter grow, too. But its
value remains immeasurable—because
there are few things in life as important as
joy, friends, and the sound of laughter.

Best Times

My best times are the
times I spend with you!

Roy Lessin

FRIENDS MAKE LIFE FUN

I cannot even imagine where I
would be today were it not for that
handful of friends who have given
me a heart full of joy. Let's face it,
friends make life a lot more fun.

CHARLES R. SWINDOLL

God Made Hugs

Everyone was meant to share
God's all-abiding love and care;
He saw that we would need to
know a way to let these feelings
show. . .so God made hugs.

JILL WOLF

A HAPPY LIFE

Friends are necessary to a happy life.

HARRY EMERSON FOSDICK

MOST EMBARRASSING MOMENT

The highlight of a "most embarrassing moment" is talking and laughing about it with our girlfriends.

CHARMING GARDENERS

Let us be grateful to people who make us
happy; they are the charming gardeners
who make our souls blossom.

MARCEL PROUST

The World Is a Rose

The world is a rose: smell it and
pass it on to your friends.

PERSIAN PROVERB

NEVER TOO WISE
FOR LAUGHTER

One should take good care not
to grow too wise for so great a
pleasure of life as laughter.

JOSEPH ADDISON

Laughter and Love

There is nothing worth the
wear of winning but laughter
and the love of friends.

HILAIRE BELLOC

One of Life's Sweetest Joys

Girlfriends are for leaning on—laughing
with—and confiding in. They are one of
the sweetest joys of life.

GOD'S GIFT

The friend given you by circumstances
over which you have no control
was God's own gift.

FREDERICK ROBERTSON

A COZY SHELTER

Friendship is a cozy shelter
from life's rainy days.

UNKNOWN

Old Friends

It is one of the blessings of
old friends that you can afford
to be stupid with them.

RALPH WALDO EMERSON

Day
88

HAPPY THOUGHTS

A happy thought shared turns an ordinary
day into one that shines in your memory.

UNKNOWN

Memories

Memories filled with laughter
are the ones we tend to recall
over and over again. They hold
the unique ability to be just
as much fun (sometimes even
more!) on the "replay."

BLESSINGS COME. . .

Blessings come in many ways.

The nicest come as friends.

THE BEST IN ME

I love you for the part of
me you bring out.

ELIZABETH BARRETT BROWNING

"Do You Remember—?"

A girlfriend is someone to whom
you can say, "Do you remember—?"
And within seconds you are both
laughing hysterically.

Spread Kindness

Do not keep the alabaster boxes
of your kindness sealed up until
your friends are gone.
Speak approving, cheering words
while their ears can hear them—
and be made happier by them.

GEORGE WILLIAM CHILDS

BRINGING JOY

Bringing joy to a friend is one
of life's greatest pleasures.

Strengthened

I cannot count the number of
times I have been strengthened
by another woman's heartfelt hug,
appreciative note, surprise gift,
or caring questions.

DEE BRESTIN

THE PUREST GIFT

I have learned that to have a good friend
is the purest of all God's gifts, for it is a
love that has no exchange of payment.

FRANCES FARMER

A LITTLE TIME

A little time for laughter,
A little time to sing,
A little time to be with friends
Will cure most anything.

Day
98

GIFT OF MAKING FRIENDS

Blessed are they who have
the gift of making friends,
for it is one of God's best gifts.

THOMAS HUGHES

Solace and Joy

A friend is a solace in grief and
in joy a merry companion.

JOHN LYLY

Day
100

I Thank God for You

*I thank my God upon
every remembrance of you.*

<small>Philippians 1:3 kjv</small>

Girlfriends Just Know

Girlfriends just know—you
can't go shopping for a bathing
suit after lunch without giggling
(in mock-horror) in the dressing
room about the snug fit.

ONE SPECIAL FRIEND

There is one friend in the life of each
of us who seems not a separate person,
however dear and beloved, but an
expansion, an interpretation, of one's self,
the very meaning of one's soul.

EDITH WHARTON

THE GREATEST TREASURE

After the friendship of God,
a friend's affection is the
greatest treasure here below.

UNKNOWN

Day
104

A Rare Book

A friend is a rare book of which
but one copy is made.

UNKNOWN

Happy Time

Girlfriend time is happy time.

WHAT WE SHARE

Friendship is not created by what we give,
but more by what we share. It makes a
whole world of things easier to bear.

UNKNOWN

Close Friends

Close friends contribute to our
personal growth. They also
contribute to our personal pleasure,
making the music sound sweeter,
the wine taste richer, the laughter
ring louder because they are there.

JUDITH VIORST

VALUE EACH DAY

Teach me, Father, to value each day,
to live, to love, to laugh, to play.

KATHI MILLS

STRIVE TO HAVE FRIENDS

Strive to have friends, for life without
friends is like life on a desert island.

BALTASAR GRACIAN

GIRLFRIENDS UNDERSTAND EVERYTHING

Girlfriends understand the healing
properties of laughter, chocolate,
and a good, long shopping trip.

The Language of Friendship

The language of friendship is
not words but meanings.

HENRY DAVID THOREAU

Day
112

THE HOPE OF THE HEART

A friend is the hope of the heart.

RALPH WALDO EMERSON

To Love and Be Loved

Life is to be fortified by
many friendships. To love and
to be loved is the greatest
happiness of existence.

SYDNEY SMITH

FOUR-LEAF CLOVER

A best friend is like a four-leaf clover:
hard to find and lucky to have.

UNKNOWN

TEARS AND LAUGHTER

Girlfriends are the ones you can
laugh *and* cry with—sometimes
in the same conversation.

I Go to My Friends

Some people go to priests;
others to poetry; I to my friends.

Virginia Woolf

Footprints

Many people will walk in and out
of your life, but only true friends
will leave footprints in your heart.

ELEANOR ROOSEVELT

LOVE OF TRUE FRIENDS

When you ask God for a gift,
be thankful if He sends,
not diamonds, pearls, or riches,
but the love of real true friends.

HELEN STEINER RICE

Celebrate Living

Celebrate the happiness that friends
are always giving; make every day a
holiday and celebrate just living!

AMANDA BRADLEY

Joy Doubled

Friendship improves happiness
and abates misery by doubling
our joys and dividing our grief.

Joseph Addison

HELLO!

A friend, in one *hello*
over the phone, can make you
feel better than ten minutes of
conversation with anyone else.

HUMOR, PRESERVED

Humor is a serious thing.
I like to think of it as one of our
greatest earliest natural resources,
which must be preserved at all cost.

JAMES THURBER

Preservatives

Good humor is one of the
preservatives of our peace
and tranquility.

THOMAS JEFFERSON

Sisters

We've shared so much laughter,
so many tears. We have a spiritual
bond that grows stronger each year.
We're not sisters by birth, but we
knew from the start, something put
us together to be sisters by heart.

Unknown

Kind Hearts

There are kind hearts still
for friends to fill.

Robert Louis Stevenson

Most Important Ships

There are many types of ships. There are
wooden ships, plastic ships, and metal
ships. But the best and most important
type of ships are friendships.

Old Irish Quote

Walking with a Friend

Walking with a friend in
the dark is better than
walking alone in the light.

HELEN KELLER

SPECIAL ABILITIES

*Each one should use whatever
gift he has received to serve others,
faithfully administering God's
grace in its various forms.*

1 PETER 4:10 NIV

Never-Ending Joy

Girlfriends just know—the gift of
laughter brings never-ending joy.

Friends Are Angels

Friends are the angels who lift us to
our feet when our wings have trouble
remembering how to fly.

Unknown

THE SONG IN YOUR HEART

A friend hears the song in my heart and
sings it to me when my memory fails.

UNKNOWN

Day
134

HAPPY BENEFITS

There is no duty we so underrate as the
duty of being happy. By being happy
we sow benefits upon the world.

ROBERT LOUIS STEVENSON

A Special Place

We should give laughter a place in
each of our days—and girlfriends
a special place in our hearts.

ANGEL KISSES

Friends are kisses blown

to us by angels.

UNKNOWN

Refreshed

In the sweetness of friendship let there be laughter, and sharing of pleasures. For in the dew of little things the heart finds its morning and is refreshed.

KAHLIL GIBRAN

THE SAVING THING

Humor is the great thing, the saving thing.
The minute it crops up, all our irritation
and resentments slip away, and a sunny
spirit takes their place.

MARK TWAIN

WHO ELSE BUT A GIRLFRIEND?

Who else but a girlfriend can laugh out
loud at something insane and exclaim in
the same breath, "That's not funny!"

WHO INVENTED GIGGLING?

It's a given—
girlfriends invented giggling.

Heart-Warmers

True friends warm the
heart and make us laugh.

No Better Feelings

There are no better feelings in life than
the feelings you experience when you are
surrounded by the friends you love.

Unknown

No Matter What

Loves may come and go but friends
are forever, no matter what.

UNKNOWN

Just Me

Girlfriend motto: If you want a hug,
I'll be your pillow. If you need to be
happy, I'll be your smile.
But anytime you need a friend,
I'll just be me.

BE WELL

Laugh and be well.

M. GREEN

A Life Worthwhile

To laugh a bit and joke a bit
and grasp a friendly hand. . .
To tell one's secrets, hopes,
and fears and share a friendly smile;
To have a friend and be a friend
is what makes life worthwhile.

Unknown

The Road to Happiness

Take time to be friendly—
it is the road to happiness.

UNKNOWN

SACRED LAUGHTER

It is often just as sacred to
laugh as it is to pray.

CHARLES R. SWINDOLL

Invisible Golden Bow

Friendship is a gift tied with
an invisible golden bow.

UNKNOWN

JOIN IN!

Joining in the laughter and delighting in the humor of life with girlfriends easily invigorates spirits and lightens souls.

WHAT IS A FRIEND?

A friend is someone you can do
nothing with—and really enjoy it.

THE BEST

That is the best—to laugh with
someone because you both think
the same things are funny.

GLORIA VANDERBILT

Loyal Friends

A loyal friend laughs at your jokes
when they're not so good,
and sympathizes with your
problems when they're not so bad.

Arnold H. Glasgow

Day
154

LAUGHTER MAKES US HAPPY

We don't laugh because we're happy—
we're happy because we laugh.

WILLIAM JAMES

A Friendly Smile

A friendly smile makes you happy.

PROVERBS 15:30 CEV

LITTLE DEEDS OF KINDNESS

Little deeds of kindness, little words
of love, help to make earth happy
like the heaven above.

J. FLETCHER-CARNEY

SURVIVAL KIT

Every survival kit should
include a sense of humor.

UNKNOWN

THE SOUND WE
LOVE TO HEAR

There's something wonderful about
making our girlfriends laugh.
Maybe it's the sound we love to hear—
or the joy we feel in brightening their
world for just a moment.

The Sensation
of Laughter

Laughter is the sensation of feeling
good all over and showing it
principally in one place.

JOSH BILLINGS

Day
160

MUSIC TO THE SOUL

Laughter among girlfriends
is music to the soul.

A Cheerful Word

Worry weighs us down;
a cheerful word picks us up.

PROVERBS 12:25 MSG

BRING ON THE CHOCOLATE!

Girlfriends just know—nothing beats
laughing about ex-boyfriends while
sharing a box (or two) of chocolate.

CHERISHED FRIENDS

We cherish our friends not
for their ability to amuse us,
but for ours to amuse them.

EVELYN WAUGH

TELL IT LIKE IT IS!

A friend doesn't go on a diet because you
are fat. A friend never defends a husband
who gets his wife an electric skillet for her
birthday. A friend will tell you she saw
your old boyfriend and he's a priest.

ERMA BOMBECK

Most Pleasant Sound

The most pleasant sound on earth
is the laughter of good friends.

MEMORIES

Memories wrapped in
laughter are a joy to reopen.

Defense

Humor is just another defense
against the universe.

MEL BROOKS

The Joy of Friendship

Words cannot express the joy which
a friend imparts; they only can know
who have experienced that joy.

Saint John Chrysostom

ONE OF LIFE'S BEST TREATS

To be surrounded by girlfriends
that make you laugh every day:
that is one of life's best treats.

Day
170

REFRESHING!

Reliable friends who do what they say are like cool drinks in sweltering heat—refreshing!

PROVERBS 25:13 MSG

Enjoy Each Day

Unless each day can be looked
back upon by an individual as one
in which she has had some fun,
some joy, some real satisfaction,
that day is a loss.

UNKNOWN

Day
172

Sweetener of Life

Friendship!

Mysterious cement of the soul!

Sweetener of life!

Robert Blair

Bubbles of Laughter

A smile starts on the lips,
a grin spreads to the eyes,
a chuckle comes from the belly;
but a good laugh bursts forth from the
soul, overflows, and bubbles all around.

CAROLYN BIRMINGHAM

GIRLFRIENDS ARE DEPENDABLE

You can always count on your
girlfriends to make you laugh so
hard soda comes out of your nose.

THE BEST SUPPORT SYSTEM

Girlfriends provide the best
support system by helping us
laugh through our troubles.

Day
176

Enjoy It

If you can eat today, enjoy the sunlight
today, mix good cheer with friends today,
enjoy it and bless God for it.

Henry Ward Beecher

The Chocolate Chips of Life

In the cookies of life, girlfriends
are the chocolate chips!

UNKNOWN

Day
178

LIFE'S ENGINE

The sense of humor is the oil of life's engine. Without it, the machinery creaks and groans. No lot is so hard, no aspect of things is so grim, but it relaxes before a hearty laugh.

GEORGE S. MERRIAM

Laughter and Health

People who laugh actually live
longer than those who don't laugh.
Few persons realize that health
actually varies according to the
amount of laughter.

JAMES J. WALSH

JUST THE BEGINNING

A smile is never an ending but
always a beautiful beginning.

UNKNOWN

A Daily Resolution

When you rise in the morning,
form a resolution to make the day
a happy one to a fellow friend.

S. Smith

FLOWERS OF JOY

Seeds of friendship
bring flowers of joy.

Multiply Joy

Friendships multiply joys.

THOMAS FULLER

THINGS THAT MAKE
LIFE WORTHWHILE

I believe there are two things in
this world that make life worth living:
laughter and good friends.

Good and Supportive

A best friend is like a good bra:
close to your heart, hard to find,
and supportive.

UNKNOWN

A GOOD LAUGH

A good laugh is
sunshine in a house.

UNKNOWN

A TREASURE

Laughter between girlfriends
is a treasure worth more than
gold or precious stones.

THE BOND OF FRIENDSHIP

I may have chosen my friends,
but the strength of the bond between
us was beyond my control.

ANITA WIEGAND

Life without Laughter

Total absence of humor
renders life impossible.

COLETTE

WHAT A LAUGH CAN DO

I have seen what a laugh can do.
It can transform almost unbearable tears
into something bearable, even hopeful.

BOB HOPE

Forever Love

A friend loveth at all times.

PROVERBS 17:17 KJV

THE LITTLE THINGS

Girlfriends just know—it's the chick flicks
you watch together, the junk food you eat
together, the things you laugh at together
that make friendship a joy.

To Laugh and Love

Laugh as much as you breathe
and love as long as you live.

THE GOLDEN THREAD

There is in friendship something of all
relations, and something above them all.
It is the golden thread that ties the
hearts of all the world.

JOHN EVELYN

Friendship Warms the World

Friends warm the
world with happiness.

UNKNOWN

THE BEST IN ME

My best friend is the one who
brings out the best in me.

HENRY FORD

Thank God for Girlfriends

I thank God for my girlfriends, for the blessing they are, for the joy of their laughter, the comfort of their prayers, and the warmth of their smiles.

A Gratuitous Joy

Friendship ought to be a gratuitous joy,
like the joys afforded by art,
or life (like aesthetic joys).

Simone Weil

A Good Belly Laugh

Girlfriends never expect anything
but a good belly laugh.

Day
200

THE SONG IN YOUR HEART

A friend is someone who knows the song
in your heart and can sing it back to you
when you have forgotten the words.

UNKNOWN

Girlfriends Find the Humor

No matter what kind of disaster takes place, girlfriends find ways to turn the seemingly serious into the most humorous situations ever.

Day
202

HEART TREASURES

If we had all the riches that we could
ever spend, it could never buy the
treasures the heart finds in a friend.

UNKNOWN

Live Better

Laughter helps us live
better and longer.

EFFECTIVE WEAPON

The human race has one really effective
weapon, and that is laughter.

MARK TWAIN

BETTER STILL

The sweet smell of incense can make you feel good, but true friendship is better still.

PROVERBS 27:9 CEV

Unique Capacity

God equips our girlfriends with the
unique capacity to lighten difficult
circumstances with a little laughter
and lots of encouragement.

The Most
Civilized Music

Laughter is the most civilized
music in the world.

PETER USTINOV

SHOCK ABSORBER

Laughter is the shock absorber
that eases the blows of life.

The Source of Pleasure

Friendship is the source of the
greatest pleasures, and without
friends even the most agreeable
pursuits become tedious.

SIR THOMAS AQUINAS

Not Far

You never have to look far to
find a reason to share happiness.

Unknown

THE GREATEST HAPPINESS

That action is best which
procures the greatest happiness
for the greatest numbers.

FRANCIS HUTCHESON

Day
212

FULL VALUE OF JOY

To get the full value of joy you must
have somebody to divide it with.

MARK TWAIN

Express Your Love

To feel love gives pleasure to one;
to express it gives pleasure to two.

JANETTE OKE

A HEARTY LAUGH

Sharing a long and hearty
laugh with your girlfriends
brings pleasure and healing.

Precious

Friendship is precious,
not only in the shade,
but in the sunshine of life.

THOMAS JEFFERSON

PRIVILEGE OF FRIENDSHIP

'Tis the privilege of friendship
to talk nonsense, and have
her nonsense respected.

CHARLES LAMB

Unshared Joy

Unshared joy is an unlighted candle.

Spanish Proverb

FRIENDS ARE THERMOMETERS

When the sun shines on you,
you see your friends. Friends are the
thermometers by which one may judge
the temperature of our fortunes.

MARGUERITE BLESSINGTON

Count Your Blessings

When we count the blessings
God has given, we should count
our friends twice—and those who
bring us laughter, twice more.

THE BEGINNING OF FRIENDSHIP

We cannot tell the precise moment
when friendship is formed. As in filling
a vessel drop by drop, there is at last
a drop which makes it run over.

JAMES BOSWELL

The House of a Friend

I find happiness, peace,
and heart's content when I
enter the house of a friend.

UNKNOWN

BE KIND

*Be kindly affectionate one to another. . .
in honour preferring one another.*

ROMANS 12:10 KJV

COMICAL TIMES

Girlfriends just know—the most
embarrassing times can easily turn
into the most comical times when
describing it to the girls.

GENUINE FRIENDS

Genuine friends can enter into
our celebration with as much or
more enthusiasm as they would
have if the fortuitous serendipity
had happened to them.

LLOYD JOHN OGILVIE

A World with No Sun

What sweetness is left in life if
you take away friendship? It is like
robbing the world of the sun.

Marcus Tullius Cicero

NEVER IN THE WAY

A true friend never gets in your way
unless you happen to be going down.

ARNOLD GLASOW

Be Wise!

Laugh, if you are wise.

LATIN PROVERB

A Best Friend and Chocolate

There's nothing better than a best friend,
except a best friend with chocolate.

THE GOLDEN CIRCLE

If you truly love and enjoy your
friends they are a part of the golden
circle that makes life good.

MARJORIE HOLMES

Friends Are Like Melons

Friends are like melons; shall I tell you why? To find one good you must one hundred try.

Claude Monet

Wear a Smile

Wear a smile and have friends.

GEORGE ELIOT

FASHIONABLE

It is a comely fashion to be glad—
Joy is the grace we say to God.

JEAN INGELOW

Get a Good Grasp of Life

A sense of humor. . .is needed
armor. Joy in one's heart and some
laughter on one's lips is a sign that
the person down deep has a pretty
good grasp of life.

HUGH SIDEY

Everyone Has a Gift

Every one has a gift for something,
even if it is the gift of being a good friend.

Marian Anderson

LIFESAVERS

With a friend you can face the worst.
Can you round up a third?
A three-stranded rope
isn't easily snapped.

ECCLESIASTES 4:12 MSG

NOTHING IS GREATER
THAN FRIENDSHIP

I keep my friends as misers do their
treasure, because, of all the things
granted us by wisdom, none is
greater or better than friendship.

PIETRO ARETINO

Good Friends

I count myself in nothing
else so happy as in a soul
remembering my good friends.

WILLIAM SHAKESPEARE

My Well-Spring

Best friend, my well-spring
in the wilderness.

George Eliot

The Finest Sound

I have always felt that laughter in
the face of reality is probably the
finest sound there is and will last
until the day when the game is
called on account of darkness.
In this world, a good time to laugh
is any time you can.

LINDA ELLERBEE

"Celebrate!"

Celebrate and be glad forever!
I am creating a Jerusalem,
full of happy people.

Isaiah 65:18 CEV

No Regrets

You'll never regret sharing
a smile with a friend.

UNKNOWN

LAUGHTER AND CONVERSATION

With girlfriends, laughter usually
outlasts the conversation.

Full of Surprises

Humor is a spontaneous,
wonderful bit of an outburst that
just comes. It's unbridled,
it's unplanned, it's full of surprises.

ERMA BOMBECK

MORE TIME FOR LAUGHTER

Make more time to
laugh with your friends;
you'll be better because of it.

All Agree

Friendship is the only thing in the
world concerning the usefulness of
which all mankind are agreed.

MARCUS TULLIUS CICERO

MANKIND'S GREATEST BLESSING

Humor is mankind's greatest blessing.

MARK TWAIN

LAUGHTER IN FLOWERS

Earth laughs in flowers.

RALPH WALDO EMERSON

SOMETHING. . .OR NOTHING?

Girlfriends always seem to find something
to laugh about—and they also find it
pretty easy to laugh about nothing at all.

Best Friends

A stranger stabs you in the front;
a friend stabs you in the back;
a boyfriend stabs you in the heart;
but best friends only poke each
other with straws.

UNKNOWN

Day
250

FEEL JOY

Learn how to feel joy.

SENECA

Day
251

A Keeper

To find one real friend in
a lifetime is good fortune;
to keep him is a blessing.

BALTASAR GRACIAN

FRIENDS STAND BY EACH OTHER

Friends stand by each other through thick and thin; every time you need me I will always be there for you. You make me happy, you make me laugh, and you are the best friend anyone could ever have.

UNKNOWN

Soul Refreshment

*A sweet friendship
refreshes the soul.*

Proverbs 27:9 MSG

TWO GREAT
PLEASURES IN LIFE

Girlfriends just know—two of the greatest
pleasures in life are having a lot of fun
and laughing harder than anything.

A Friend Is Dearer

A friend is dearer than the
light of heaven, for it would be
better for us that the sun were
extinguished than that we
should be without friends.

SAINT JOHN CHRYSOSTOM

HAPPIEST BUSINESS

The happiest business in all the
world is that of making friends,
and he who gives in friendship's
name shall reap what he has spent.

ANNE S. EATON

Kind Words

Many a friendship—
long, loyal, and self-sacrificing—
rested at first upon no thicker a
foundation than a kind word.

FREDERICK W. FABER

DOUBLY BLESSED

Girlfriends are blessed doubly
when their gab sessions are
interrupted by laughter.

COMFORTING

Friendship is a very
comforting thing to have.

A. A. MILNE

A SECRET

The greatest sweetener of human
life is friendship. To raise this to the
highest pitch of enjoyment is a secret
which but few discover.

JOSEPH ADDISON

"Remember When"

Let's become little old ladies
together—we'll stay up late looking
at old pictures, telling "remember
when" stories, and laughing
till our sides ache.

Unknown

Day
262

TO BE PRIZED

There is nothing on this earth more
to be prized than true friendship.

SIR THOMAS AQUINAS

They Understand

Good friends help us maintain a
healthy sense of humor. When
we need to laugh at ourselves,
they make us feel like it's okay. .
.and because they understand, it's
never offensive when they join in.

POWER OF SHARED LAUGHTER

One can never speak enough
of the virtues, the dangers,
the power of shared laughter.

FRANÇOISE SAGAN

THE RULE OF FRIENDSHIP

The rule of friendship means there
should be mutual sympathy between
them, each supplying what the other lacks
and trying to benefit the other,
always using friendly and sincere words.

MARCUS TULLIUS CICERO

PLAY, LAUGHTER, AND JOY

Your body cannot heal without play.
Your mind cannot heal without laughter.
Your soul cannot heal without joy.

CATHERINE FENWICK

A Looking-Glass

The world is a looking-glass,
and gives back to every man the
reflection of his own face. Frown at
it, and it in turn will look sourly at
you; laugh at it, and with it, and it
is a jolly, kind companion.

WILLIAM THACKERAY

EFFORTLESS MELODY

Laughter flows in a violent
riff and is effortlessly melodic.

Laughing, Trusting, and Caring

Friendship is sharing openly,
laughing often, trusting always,
caring deeply.

UNKNOWN

An Oasis

My friends are an oasis to me,
encouraging me to go on.
They are essential to my well-being.

Dee Brestin

ENJOY LIFE AS LONG AS YOU CAN

There is nothing better than to be happy
and enjoy ourselves as long as we can.

ECCLESIASTES 3:12 NLT

Day
272

FROM A JOYOUS HEART

A laugh, to be joyous, must flow
from a joyous heart, for without
kindness, there can be no true joy.

THOMAS CARLYLE

The Common
Denominator

Among those whom I like or
admire, I can find no common
denominator, but among those
whom I love, I can: All of them
make me laugh.

W. H. AUDEN

Day
274

THE BETTER PART OF LIFE

The better part of one's
life consists of his friendships.

ABRAHAM LINCOLN

Happiness Is. . .

Happiness is time spent with
a friend and looking forward
to time with them again.

LEE WILKINSON

LAUGHTER TO LIFE

Best friends bring laughter to life.

MEMORIES OF TOMORROW

Each happiness of yesterday
is a memory of tomorrow.

GEORGE WEBSTER DOUGLAS

THOSE MOMENTS

We occasionally have moments
when we're perfectly content to feel
gloomy. . . . Then along comes a friend
who manages to encourage a smile and
can even send you into a fit of laughter.

ANITA WIEGAND

A Sunny Day

A cheerful friend is like a
sunny day, which sheds its
brightness on all around.

Sir John Lubbock

THE SWEETEST LIVES

The sweetest lives are those
that bring laughter to others.

Day
281

Happiness Shared

Happiness held is the seed;
happiness shared is the flower.

RICHLY BLESSED

A life richly blessed is one
encircled by true friends.

My Dear Friends

My dear, dear friends! . . .
You make me feel such joy.

Philippians 4:1 MSG

Day
284

THE JOYS OF A LIFETIME

Girlfriends just know—favorite people,
favorite places, favorite memories of the
past. These are the joys of a lifetime.

Heart Measurements

A friend is a gift whose
worth cannot be measured
except by the heart.

UNKNOWN

Day
286

A Little Love

Give a friend a little love and you
gain a great deal in return.

Unknown

Finding Joy

To be able to find joy in another's
joy, that is the secret of happiness.

GEORGE BERNANOS

"Spirit-Lifters"

We all need lunch breaks with
our girlfriends. It's like inserting a
"spirit-lifter" in the middle of our day.

DISCOVER JOY

Hold a hand that needs you
and discover abundant joy.

FLAVIA WEEDN

WHAT MAKES FRIENDS

Fellowship in joy,
not sympathy in sorrow,
is what makes friends.

FRIEDRICH NIETZSCHE

Smoother Pathways

Humor makes our heavy burdens
light and smooths the rough
spots in our pathways.

SAM ERVIN

THE IDEAL OF HAPPINESS

Life in common among people who love
each other is the ideal of happiness.

GEORGE SAND

The Remedy for Sorrow

Laughter is a remedy
for every sorrow.

SUPREME HAPPINESS

The supreme happiness of life is the
conviction that we are loved, loved for
ourselves, or rather in spite of ourselves.

VICTOR HUGO

Discover Friendship

How rare and wonderful is that
flash of a moment when we realize
we have discovered a friend.

William Rotsler

WHAT GREATER THING IN LIFE. . .

What greater thing is there for two human souls than to feel that they are joined together—to share with each other in all gladness?

GEORGE ELIOT

The Greatest Blessing

A friend is the greatest
of all blessings.

FRANÇOIS DE LA ROCHEFOUCAULD

Day
298

THE SHORTEST DISTANCE

Laughter is the shortest
distance between two people.

VICTOR BORGE

What Is a Friend?

What is a friend? A single soul
dwelling in two bodies.

ARISTOTLE

OPEN DOORS

Happiness is something that comes
into our lives through doors we
don't even remember leaving open.

ROSE WILDER LANE

FRIENDSHIP PROMOTES HAPPINESS

Friendship is a strong and habitual
inclination in two persons to promote the
good and happiness of one another.

EUSTACE BUDGELL

HEARTS ARE JOINED

The hearts of friends are
never so quickly joined as
when they laugh together.

Cheap Medicine

Always laugh when you can.
It is cheap medicine.

LORD BYRON

THE BEST BEGINNING AND ENDING

Laughter is not at all a bad
beginning for a friendship,
and it is far the best ending for one.

OSCAR WILDE

Like Stars

Girlfriends are like stars. You don't
always see them, but you know
they are always there.

TOUCHED WITH JOY

When hands reach out with friendship,
hearts are touched with joy.

THE INNER SPIRIT

In everyone's life, at some time, our inner
fire goes out. It is then burst into flame by
an encounter with another human being.
We should all be thankful for those people
who rekindle the inner spirit.

ALBERT SCHWEITZER

WE NEED FRIENDS

I could do without many things with no
hardship—you are not one of them.

ASHLEIGH BRILLIANT

Goodness

Cheerfulness is the
offshoot of goodness.

CHRISTIAN NESTELL BOVEE

TOUCHED BY KINDNESS

How beautiful a day can be when
kindness touches it.

UNKNOWN

The Best Things

The best and most beautiful
things in the world cannot
be seen or even touched.
They must be felt with the heart.

HELEN KELLER

CLOSER THAN FAMILY

*There is a friend that sticketh
closer than a brother.*

PROVERBS 18:24 KJV

HAPPINESS IS A BUTTERFLY

Happiness is a butterfly, which,
when pursued, is always just beyond
your grasp, but which, if you will sit
down quietly, may alight upon you.

NATHANIEL HAWTHORNE

To Have a Friend

*You are better off to have a friend than
to be all alone, because then you will get
more enjoyment out of what you earn.
If you fall, your friend can help you up.*

ECCLESIASTES 4:9–10 CEV

A Worthwhile Ride

Girlfriends just know—
friends and laughter make
the ride of life worthwhile.

Day
316

ALWAYS A FRIEND

Never shall I forget the days I spent
with you. Continue to be my friend,
as you will always find me yours.

LUDWIG VAN BEETHOVEN

The Most Rewarding Moments

Some of the most rewarding and beautiful moments of a friendship happen in the unforeseen open spaces between planned activities. It is important that we allow these spaces to exist.

COLLENBACH

Through Love and Loyalty

Friendship is a gift from God
That's blessed in every part
Born through love and loyalty
Conceived within the heart.

Unknown

"I CAN'T STOP LAUGHING"

Ever notice that when you have one of
those "I can't stop laughing" episodes,
there's usually a girlfriend involved?

Reasons We're Best Friends

It's the times we gorge on chocolate
and think we'll die. It's the times we
laugh so hard, we can't help but cry.
It's all the inside jokes and "remember
whens." Those are all the reasons
that we're best friends!

Day
321

Acquisition of Friends

Of all the means to insure
happiness throughout the whole
of life, by far the most important
is the acquisition of friends.

EPICURUS

THE SUREST WAY
TO HAPPINESS

The surest way to be happy is
to seek happiness for others.

MARTIN LUTHER KING JR.

Day
323

Sweep Away...

Laughter is the brush that sweeps
away the cobwebs of the heart.

MORT WALKER

LET THE WRINKLES COME!

With mirth and laughter
let old wrinkles come.

WILLIAM SHAKESPEARE

THE HUMOROUS SIDE

With our girlfriends it is easier to
see the humorous side of life.

HAPPINESS COMES. . .

Happiness comes of the capacity
to feel deeply, to enjoy simply,
to think freely, to risk life, to be needed.

STORM JAMESON

The Most
Marvelous Gift

Humor is one of God's
most marvelous gifts.

Sam Ervin

WHERE YOUR PLEASURE IS

Where your pleasure is,
there is your treasure;
where your treasure,
there your heart;
where your heart,
there your happiness.

SAINT AUGUSTINE

Good for the Soul

God gives the blessings of
friendship and laughter;
they're both good for the soul.

UNEXPECTED SPARKS

Our brightest blazes of gladness are
commonly kindled by unexpected sparks.

SAMUEL JOHNSON

KEEP IT SIMPLE

It's the simple things in life that make living
worthwhile, the sweet fundamental things
like love, laughter, and good friends.

A WARM WORLD

Girlfriends warm the
world with laughter.

Laugh!

If you can't make it better,
you can laugh at it.

ERMA BOMBECK

SILLINESS

Silliness is a by-product
of having girlfriends.

Day
335

Expressions of Joy

Our friends are ongoing
expressions of heaven's joy.

THINGS THAT MAKE
ME SMILE

Thinking about the times spent with my
girlfriends always makes me smile.

WET CEMENT

Friendship is like standing on wet cement.
The longer you stay, the harder it is to
leave, and you can never go without
leaving your footprints behind.

UNKNOWN

DEFINITION

Friend: One who knows all about
you and loves you just the same.

ELBERT HUBBARD

No Sweeter Sound

Is there a sweeter sound than good
friends laughing together?

SHARE THE VISION

O Lord, share with me the vision to find
joy everywhere: in the wild violet's beauty,
in the lark's melody, in a child's smile,
in a mother's love, in the purity of Jesus.

CELTIC PRAYER

In Everything Rejoice

There is not one blade of grass,
there is no color in the world that is
not intended to make us rejoice.

JOHN CALVIN

The Definition of a Smile

Smile: a curve that can
set a lot of things straight.

FRIENDS AND LAUGHTER

The path that leads to joy is
filled with friends and laughter.

FILLED WITH JOY

*The Lord has done great things for us,
and we are filled with joy.*

Psalm 126:3 niv

Pure Joy

Girlfriends just know—
Laughter + Girlfriends = Pure Joy

A FOUNTAIN OF GLADNESS

A kind heart is a fountain of gladness,
making everything in its vicinity
freshen into smiles.

WASHINGTON IRVING

A Perfume

Happiness is a perfume you cannot pour on others without getting a few drops on yourself.

RALPH WALDO EMERSON

Sure Sign

Joy is the surest sign of
the presence of God.

Pierre Teilhard de Chardin

WE CAN SHARE
THE LAUGHTER

We can laugh about our children,
our grandchildren, and ourselves—
we are girlfriends.

CHEERFULNESS

Cheerfulness, like spring, opens
all the blossoms of the inward man.

JEAN PAUL RICHTER

Day
351

Good Company

With merry company,
the dreary way is endured.

SPANISH PROVERB

Day
352

LITTLE THINGS

Girlfriends remind us that the happiness
of life is made up of little things—a smile,
a hug, a moment of shared laughter.

UNKNOWN

The Road Trip

Not many things bring on laughter
like cramming all your best
girlfriends and all your favorite
snacks into the car for a road trip.
Just be sure to pull over if the
laughing gets out of control.

REMEMBER THE LAUGHTER

When we reflect on the best times
we've shared with our girlfriends,
we may forget exactly what it was we
laughed so hard about. . .but we'll
always remember the laughter.

THE HAPPY HEART

*For the happy heart,
life is a continual feast.*

PROVERBS 15:15 NLT

MAKE ME SMILE

You're the slightly cracked ornament
that always makes me smile.

UNKNOWN

Like a Christmas Tree

Friendship is like a Christmas tree,
decorated with warm memories
and shared joys.

UNKNOWN

FRIENDS ARE LIKE MUSICAL NOTES

Friends are notes to life's great songs,
a melody that carries you along.

UNKNOWN

God Gave Us Girlfriends

It's impossible to lift something
heavy and laugh at the same time.
That's why God gave us girlfriends.
The joy they bring prevents us from
carrying the weight of our burdens alone.

LIFE WITHOUT FRIENDS?

You can live without a brother,
but not without a friend.

GERMAN PROVERB

What Are Dreams Made Of?

Friendships are what our
dreams are made of.

Elsa Maxwell

SWEET AND SIMPLE

I am beginning to learn that it
is the sweet, simple things of life
which are the real ones after all.

LAURA INGALLS WILDER

Day
363

Life's Greatest Combinations

Girlfriends and uncontrollable laughter are one of life's greatest combinations—like cake and ice cream, peanut butter and jelly, and popcorn and a movie.

PLANT A SEED

Plant a seed of friendship;
reap a bouquet of happiness.

LOIS L. KAUFMAN

God's Goodness

God's goodness to us is revealed
in our friendships. They hold the
blessings we were created to enjoy
but can't possibly number—laughter,
encouragement, compassion,
generosity, forgiveness, and love.

NOTES